A Short, Illustrated History of...

SPACE EXPLORATION

Dr. Mike Goldsmith
Fellow of the Royal Astronomical Society (FRAS)

Rita Petruccioli

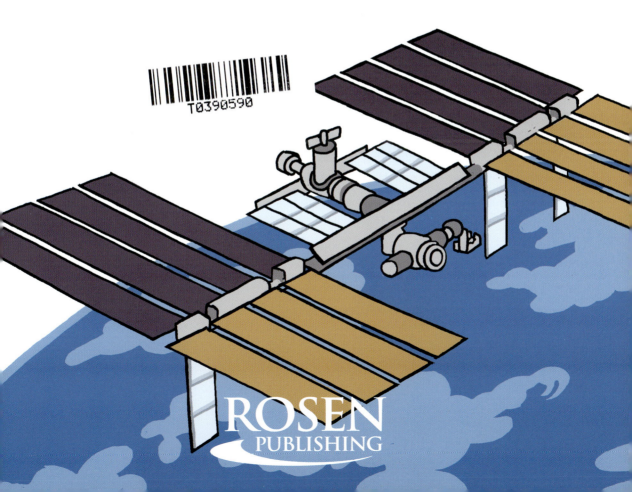

ROSEN
PUBLISHING

Published in 2025 by The Rosen Publishing Group, Inc.
2544 Clinton Street, Buffalo, NY 14224

First published in Great Britain in 2020 by The Watts Publishing Group
Copyright © The Watts Publishing Group, 2020

Series Editor: Amy Pimperton
Series Designer: Lisa Peacock
Illustrations by Rita Petruccioli

All rights reserved. No part of this book may be reproduced in any form without
permission in writing from the publisher, except by a reviewer.

The websites (URLS) included in this book were valid at the time of going to press.
However, it is possible that the contents or addresses may have changed since the
publication of this book. No responsibility for any such changes can be accepted
by either the author or the Publisher.

Cataloging-in-Publication Data

Names: Goldsmith, Mike, 1962-, author. | Petruccioli, Rita, illustrator.
Title: Space exploration / by Mike Goldsmith, illustrated by Rita Petruccioli.
Description: Buffalo, NY : Rosen Publishing, 2025. | Series: A short, illustrated
  history of... | Includes glossary and index.
Identifiers: ISBN 9781499476514 (pbk.) | ISBN 9781499476521
  (library bound) | ISBN 9781499476538 (ebook)
Subjects: LCSH: Astronomy–Juvenile literature. | Space–Juvenile literature. |
  Outer space–Juvenile literature.
Classification: LCC QB46.G64 2025 | DDC 520–dc23

Manufactured in the United States of America

CPSIA Compliance Information: Batch #CSRYA25.
For further information, contact Rosen Publishing at 1-800-237-9932.

Find us on 📘 📷

Contents

4-5 Dreaming of Space

6-7 The View from Earth

8-9 The First Space Rockets

10-11 Into Orbit

12-13 Humans in Orbit

14-15 Satellites

16-17 The Space Race

18-19 Rocket Science

20-21 Men on the Moon

22-23 Life on Mars

24-25 Missions to Mercury

26-27 Voyages to Venus

28-29 The Outer Planets

30-31 New Eyes on the Universe

32-33 A Home in Orbit

34-35 Space Shuttle

36-37 Journey to Jupiter

38-39 Saturn's Secrets

40-41 New Ways to Space

42-43 The Future in Space

44-45 Starships

46-47 Glossary/Further Information

48 Places to Visit/Index

Dreaming of Space

Space has existed for almost 14 billion years, and Earth for more than 4.5 billion years. People evolved about a quarter of a million years ago and probably have always looked up at the night sky and wondered about what they saw there. They saw that the moon and stars move across the sky during the night and change positions throughout the year.

They also noticed that five star-like objects move differently than the rest. Now we know that these objects are planets and that Earth is a planet too. All the planets move around (orbit) the sun, while the moon orbits Earth.

The moon is a world that is much nearer to us than the planets. People have always dreamed of going there. The first known story of a moon trip was written about 2,000 years ago; the travelers were the crew of a ship, thrown up into the sky by a waterspout. Later writers told stories of moon explorers who made themselves wings, harnessed geese, used giant balloons, or even shot themselves from enormous cannons.

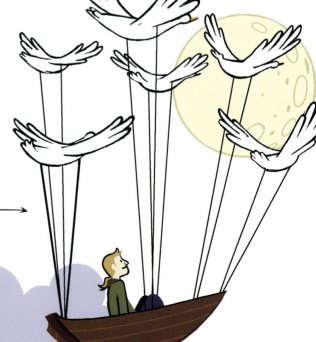

A book published in 1638 is thought to be the first work of science fiction. Called The Man in the Moone, *it features a spacecraft pulled by geese.*

In the 1880s, a Russian engineer named Konstantin Tsiolkovsky (1857–1935) realized that the secret of space travel was the rocket. Invented in ancient China thousands of years ago, rockets have been used as fireworks and weapons ever since. They are usually filled with gunpowder.

Tsiolkovsky realized that a space rocket would need a different kind of fuel: liquid fuel. In 1926, an experimental liquid-fueled rocket was launched by American engineer Robert Goddard (1882–1945). It was one step closer to humans actually visiting space.

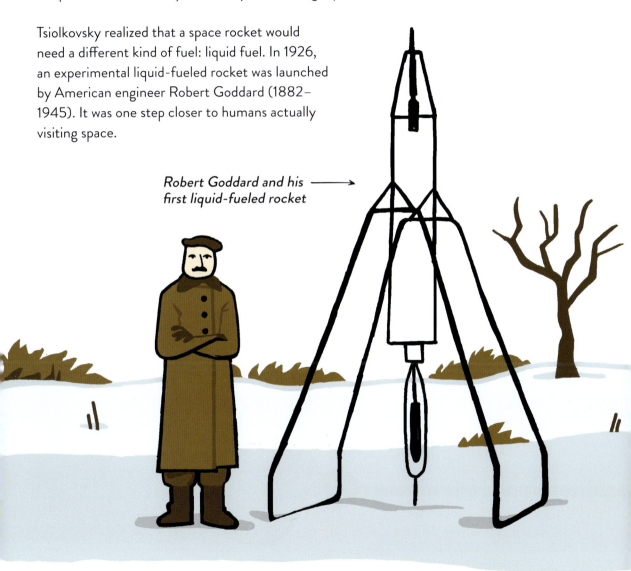

Robert Goddard and his first liquid-fueled rocket

The history of space exploration is a story full of amazing inventions, dangerous voyages, and strange discoveries. Read on to explore some of the most famous and important of these on a journey through time and space.

The View from Earth

The inventor of the first telescope is uncertain, but we do know that in 1609, the Italian scientist Galileo Galilei (1564–1642) built one of his own. By modern standards it was very poor indeed, but for Galileo it was a window to a new universe. Within a few days, he had discovered four moons around Jupiter (see pages 36–37), mountains on the moon, and hundreds of new stars.

Galileo Galilei ⟶

Galileo's telescope was the kind now called a refractor, which means that it used a glass lens to focus light. One of the problems with using a lens was that it added rainbow colors to whatever Galileo looked at. To avoid this, in 1668 English scientist Isaac Newton **(1642–1727)** built the world's first reflecting telescope, which uses a curved mirror instead of a lens to gather light.

Before Galileo, the only planets people knew of were Mercury, Venus, Mars, Jupiter, and Saturn. The development of telescopes led to the discovery of two planets much farther out in our solar system: Uranus in 1791 and Neptune in 1846.

Both reflectors and refractors are still in use today; the very largest telescopes are reflectors, and they can see the far reaches of the universe.

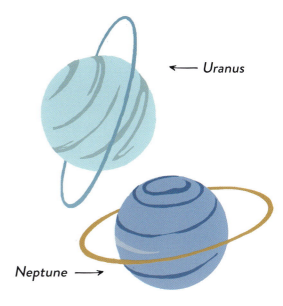

← Uranus

Neptune →

Radiation

As well as the light we can see, stars shine with many other kinds of radiation. In the early 20th century, new telescopes were invented to measure two of these kinds of invisible rays: infrared and ultraviolet. Some stars produce radio waves, too, but these can only be detected by a completely different type of telescope. In the 1950s several radio telescopes were built, including the giant Lovell Telescope at Jodrell Bank, Cheshire, England.

The Lovell Telescope was built in 1957 and is still in use today.

The First Space Rockets

In the 1930s, several groups of people in the U.S., Germany, and elsewhere began to build small rockets as a hobby, but it was the outbreak of the World War II (1939–45) that led to real breakthroughs. In rocket-making, Germany was far ahead of other countries, and in 1942 it was a German V-2 rocket that became the first spacecraft. The V-2 was a liquid-fueled war rocket, and it was on its flight to attack London that its curving path took it briefly into space.

After the war many V-2s were taken to the U.S., and their German inventor, Wernher von Braun (1912–77), went there too. Under his guidance, American scientists used the V-2s (renamed A-4s) to study the upper parts of Earth's atmosphere.

V-2 rocket →

Wernher von Braun →

The V-2s were few in number and expensive to fuel and launch, so the U.S. developed its own rockets — called Aerobees. Unlike V-2s, Aerobees were step rockets. In a step rocket, fuel tanks are discarded when they are empty, to lighten the load. The Aerobees were built in two sections, or stages. The first stage was powered by solid fuel, the second by liquid fuel. The first Aerobee blasted off in 1947. Later versions carried scientific instruments to find out more about Earth's high atmosphere. These were called sounding rockets.

Cosmic Rays

One of the things the Aerobees were used to study was cosmic rays. These mysterious bursts of particles from space are mostly blocked by Earth's atmosphere. In space, they damage both living things and electronic equipment.

When cosmic rays hit Earth's atmosphere they can produce showers of electrically charged particles.

Into Orbit

On October 4, 1957, many people around the world heard a strange beeping sound coming from their radios. The signals were sent by Sputnik 1, a spacecraft launched into space by the Soviet Union (a group of countries including Russia). At this time, the Soviet Union and the U.S. were engaged in the Cold War — a period of great tension between these two superpowers.

Sputnik was a satellite, an unmanned craft that orbits Earth. Its launch was completely unexpected, and people were shocked by it, especially in the U.S. They had been sure that the U.S. was the most technologically advanced country on Earth, and now they were worried about the military power that space control would give to the Soviet Union. Perhaps there were already bombs in orbit, under Soviet control?

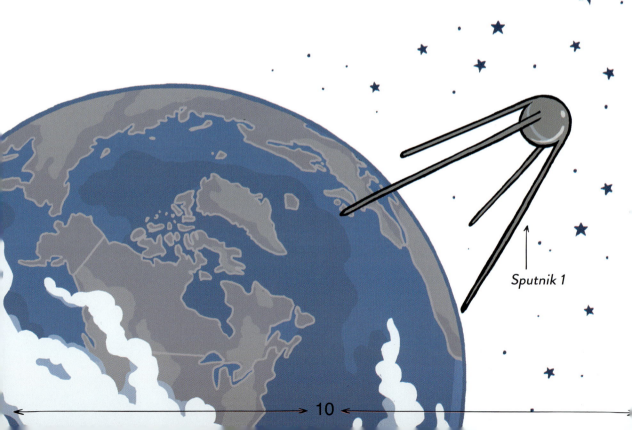

Sputnik 1

A month later, Sputnik 2 also achieved orbit, carrying with it a dog named Laika. In December the U.S. hurriedly tried to launch a satellite called Vanguard, but its rocket launcher exploded within seconds. A replacement (also called Vanguard) was successfully launched into orbit the next year. It is still in orbit today, though radio contact with it was lost in 1964.

Sadly, Laika died during her pioneering spaceflight.

Wernher von Braun (see pages 8–9) developed his V-2 rocket design to build a new rocket called Juno. In January 1958 it was used to send Explorer 1 into orbit. While Sputnik and Vanguard were designed simply to show that artificial satellites were possible, Explorer 1 lived up to its name and explored the area of space near Earth. It discovered regions of intense radiation, now called Van Allen belts, after James Van Allen (1914–2006), one of the space scientists who built the radiation-detecting instruments on Explorer 1.

Van Allen belts

Humans in Orbit

Putting people into orbit and returning them safely to Earth was much more challenging than earlier space missions. An astronaut needs protection from the extreme cold and heat of space, and this means that the space capsule in which they travel must be large and heavy. Also, the thrust of a rocket launch must be very carefully controlled; too much thrust would crush a space traveler.

It took more than three years of intense research after the launch of Sputnik before the Soviets were ready to launch a human into space. Finally, on the morning of April 12, 1961, 27-year-old Russian cosmonaut Yuri Gagarin (1934–68) was blasted into space from Kazakhstan in a spacecraft called *Vostok 1*.

Project Mercury

Meanwhile, NASA* had begun a series of missions called Project Mercury, which aimed to launch people into orbit. The first astronaut was Alan Shepard (1923–98), who piloted a spacecraft called *Freedom 7* in 1961. Shepard did not fly as high as Gagarin, nor orbit Earth. The first American who did so was John Glenn (1921–2016) in *Friendship 7*, launched in February 1962.

Soviet cosmonauts continued to hit the headlines for many years. Valentina Tereshkova (1937–) became the first woman in space in 1963, as pilot of the *Vostok 6* spacecraft.

← *Yuri Gagarin (far left) and Valentina Tereshkova (left)*

In March 1965, Alexei Leonov (1934–2019) became the first person to walk in space when he left his *Voskhod 2* capsule for a 12-minute spacewalk. Three months later, in June 1965, the first American astronaut to perform a spacewalk was Ed White (1930–67).

Alexei Leonov

* NASA stands for National Aeronautics and Space Administration. Established in the U.S. in 1958, Project Mercury was its first human spaceflight program.

13

Satellites

While the first astronauts were venturing into space, many new satellites were being developed to carry out tasks that were easier from space than from the ground.

Earth's atmosphere blocks out a whole range of radiation from the sun, stars, and planets. Telescopes on orbiting satellites are not shielded from this radiation so they could study the celestial bodies for the first time. The first such astronomy satellite was NASA's Explorer 7, launched in 1959 to study ultraviolet and X-rays from the sun.

The next year, NASA launched Tiros-1, the first successful weather satellite. With its ability to see huge areas of Earth at once, it was ideal for the monitoring of hurricanes. These storms are so huge that they can be seen fully only from space.

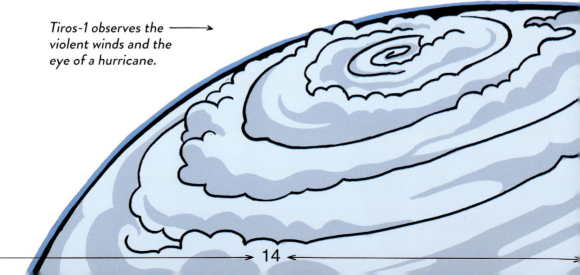

Tiros-1 observes the violent winds and the eye of a hurricane.

Parachutes and Packages

Launched by the U.S. in 1960, the first spy satellites automatically dropped the photographs they took. Parachutes slowed down the packages, and aircraft snatched them out of the air as they fell. These complicated systems were soon replaced by versions in which the picture information was sent to Earth by radio signals.

A U.S. military aircraft snared the parachute and photograph capsule as they fell to the ground.

Radio signals from satellites allow their positions to be measured with great accuracy.

Today, a system of 24 satellites called GPS (Global Positioning System) does this job, but the first such system, called Transit, went into use in 1964. It was used by the U.S. military. Satellites were soon also being used as spies in the sky, using long-range cameras to watch developments in enemy countries. There is still much secrecy around the uses and locations of some of these early spy satellites.

The Space Race

Once the Soviet Union and U.S. had learned how to launch people into space, they both decided to head for the moon, which was the ultimate goal of the Space Race. This desire to dominate space technology, innovation, and travel was a hard-fought competition between the Cold War enemies: the U.S. and the Soviet Union. Winning was a matter of national pride as well as security.

The Soviets achieved the first big success in 1959 when the unmanned Luna 2 probe reached the moon. Determined to catch up, in 1961 U.S. president John F. Kennedy (1917–63) announced his intention of landing a man on the moon before 1970.

This was a bold plan, as no one in the world knew how to achieve it. In fact, no one even knew what the moon's surface was like, so in 1964 a NASA probe called Ranger 7 was sent there to find out. Like Luna 2, it was designed to crash into the moon, but Ranger 7 was equipped with a TV camera and a radio system, so it could send back photos of the surface during its descent.

John F. Kennedy

Lunar Orbiter

Three years later another U.S. spacecraft, Lunar Orbiter, took detailed photos of the moon for explorers to use as maps.

The next goal was to land a craft on the moon, rather than smashing into it. This was achieved in 1966 by the Soviet Luna 9 probe.

Meanwhile, astronauts were learning to be moon explorers. NASA's Gemini program began in 1961 and sent ten pairs of astronauts into orbit over the next five years. The astronauts learned to spacewalk and to fly spacecraft. They also spent many hours in orbit, to make sure that humans could survive and work in the weightless conditions involved in trips to the moon.

A Gemini capsule

Twins

The constellation of Gemini represents twins. This name was chosen for the program because a Gemini capsule carried two astronauts.

Rocket Science

To take people to the moon, a far more powerful rocket than had ever been built before was needed. It had to do more than simply lift its three-man crew all the way to the moon — an average distance of 238,855 miles (384,400 km) from Earth.

A moon rocket also had to carry a return craft, together with enough air, water, and food for the eight-day journey. All this added up to a lot of weight, which meant a lot of fuel — enough to drive a car around Earth a thousand times! In fact, 97 percent of the weight of a manned moon rocket at liftoff was its fuel.

NASA moon rockets were called Saturn Vs (pronounced "fives"). They were step rockets (see page 9), and those that reached the moon had three stages. The first stage lifted the spacecraft to a height of about 42 miles (68 km). The second stage carried it to the outer edge of the atmosphere, and the third stage sent it on its way to the moon. The first two stages fell into the Atlantic Ocean. The third stages either stayed in space or fell to the moon, where they remain.

A Saturn V's first stage and the interstage (ring-shaped) adapter fall away as the second stage blasts toward space.

While the Saturn Vs were being designed and tested, NASA engineers were also developing spacesuits to keep the astronauts alive while they explored the moon. Spacesuits provided their wearers with air and water, kept them at a comfortable pressure, and also gave protection from the extreme temperatures they would encounter there.

A moon spacesuit →

Men on the Moon

On July 21, 1969, two men from Earth cautiously made their way down the ladder of their tiny landing craft and stepped onto the surface of the moon. For the first time in history, humans had touched another world.

The Apollo lunar module, Eagle, touches down on the moon.

The men were American astronauts Neil Armstrong (1930–2012) and Buzz Aldrin (1930–), and their craft was a lunar module called *Eagle*. They had spent three days traveling over 233,635 miles (376,000 km) from Cape Kennedy, Florida, to the *Mare Tranquillitatis* (Sea of Tranquility) on the moon.

Their mission was called Apollo 11, and it was the first of six moon-landing missions. In each of them, three men were blasted off Earth by a huge and powerful Saturn V rocket. As the Saturn Vs used up their fuel, they discarded the empty tanks (see pages 18–19). By the time the moon was reached, just two small modules remained. *Columbia* stayed in orbit around the moon with Michael Collins (1930–2021) on board, while *Eagle* ferried the other astronauts down to the moon and back.

On the moon, Armstrong and Aldrin collected rock samples and set up measuring instruments. One of these detected moonquakes and another helped measure the distance to Earth with great accuracy.

↑ *From left to right: Collins, Aldrin, and Armstrong*

More Moon Missions

In total, twelve astronauts have walked on the surface of the moon. The last Apollo mission returned to Earth in 1972, but more manned missions are planned for the future. Until then, a scattering of spacecraft and discarded equipment is all that remains on the moon — as well as the footprints of its first explorers.

Life on Mars

Of all the planets in our solar system, Mars is the most similar to Earth. It has seasons, clouds, icy poles, and a day of a similar length. Because of this, scientists have always hoped to find signs of living creatures there.

But Mars is a difficult world to visit; most missions there have ended in lost, failed, or crashed spacecraft. Finally, in 1965, the NASA Mariner 4 probe flew close by the planet and sent back images of its rocky cratered surface. Two more Mariner probes flew past in 1969.

In November 1971 a Soviet probe, Mars 2, crashed into the planet. A few days later Mars 3 landed successfully — but it stopped sending signals a few seconds later and was never heard from again. Meanwhile, the NASA Mariner probe was in orbit around Mars, but it could see no details through a huge dust storm that shrouded the whole planet. Finally, the storm cleared and revealed dry river beds. This showed that water was once plentiful on Mars — water is essential for living things.

The red color of Mars is caused by rust (iron oxide) in the Martian soil.

In 1976, the twin NASA Viking probes landed and carried out tests. The results were very strange, probably due to unusual chemicals in the Martian soil. Since then, several NASA robot rovers have landed successfully on Mars and more are on their way. Plentiful supplies of ice have been found (mostly underground) and occasional traces of surface water too. The search for life on Mars continues.

A Viking probe on Mars

Missions to Mercury

The sun is far more massive than all the planets put together, and that means it has an enormously strong gravitational pull. If you could stand on the sun, you would weigh over a ton. The planet Mercury is very close to the sun, where strong solar gravity pulls hard on any visiting space probes.

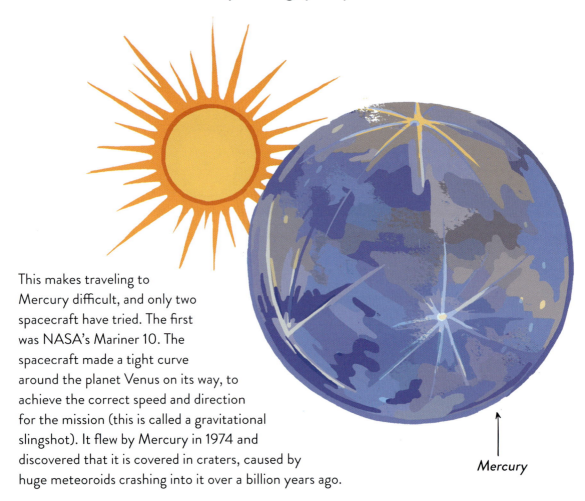

Mercury

This makes traveling to Mercury difficult, and only two spacecraft have tried. The first was NASA's Mariner 10. The spacecraft made a tight curve around the planet Venus on its way, to achieve the correct speed and direction for the mission (this is called a gravitational slingshot). It flew by Mercury in 1974 and discovered that it is covered in craters, caused by huge meteoroids crashing into it over a billion years ago.

The second Mercury probe was MESSENGER*. It swung around Venus twice and passed Mercury six times before settling into orbit in 2011. Mercury's surface is hot enough in some places to melt metal, so MESSENGER surprised everyone by finding ice there, in craters that are always in shadow. MESSENGER crash-landed on Mercury in 2015, leaving behind a small new crater.

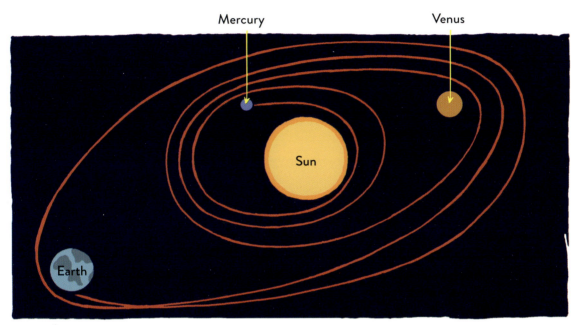

↑ *The flight path of the MESSENGER probe on its way to Mercury*

BepiColombo

A third Mercury probe was launched in 2018, by the European Space Agency (ESA) and the Japanese Aerospace Exploration Agency. It is named BepiColombo after Guiseppe "Bepi" Colombo (1920–84), the scientist who invented the gravitational slingshot maneuver. The probe is expected to reach Mercury in 2025.

* MESSENGER stands for **ME**rcury **S**urface **S**pace **EN**vironment **GE**ochemistry and **R**anging.

Voyages to Venus

Venus is the closest planet to Earth and the brightest in the night sky, but its thick clouds hide its surface from us. It is similar in size to Earth but spins clockwise on its axis. All the planets, except Venus and Uranus, spin counterclockwise.

Very little was known about the planet until 1962, when NASA's Mariner 2 probe flew by and found a very hot, dry world. Eight years later, the Soviet Venera 7 probe landed on Venus and found atmospheric pressures much higher than on Earth.

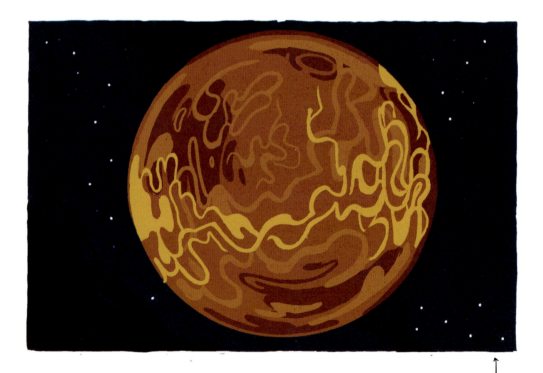

In 1975, the Venera 9 lander took the first pictures of the surface, revealing a rocky, shadowless landscape and bright clouds full of acid. Those images were black and white; it was not until 1982 that color photos were taken by the Venera 13 lander. These showed an orange-yellow world of dry rock and gravel.

Venus's thick clouds create a greenhouse effect, making it the hottest planet in the solar system.

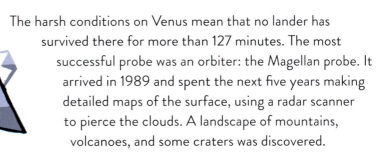

The harsh conditions on Venus mean that no lander has survived there for more than 127 minutes. The most successful probe was an orbiter: the Magellan probe. It arrived in 1989 and spent the next five years making detailed maps of the surface, using a radar scanner to pierce the clouds. A landscape of mountains, volcanoes, and some craters was discovered.

An even longer study of Venus was made by Venus Express, an ESA orbiter, which studied the atmosphere from 2005 until 2014.

Venus still holds many mysteries: lightning, active volcanoes, and even metal-coated mountain tops may all be present, but no one yet knows for sure. Another mystery is the cause of the very high wind speeds in the upper atmosphere, which carry high clouds around the planet in just four days.

Magellan probe

Around the World

The Magellan probe was named after Portuguese explorer Ferdinand Magellan (c. 1480–1521), who organized the first expedition to circumnavigate Earth. His fleet had five ships to begin with, but only one — the *Victoria* — completed the circumnavigation. Magellan died about halfway through the epic journey.

Ferdinand Magellan

The Outer Planets

There are two kinds of planets in our solar system: small rocky ones like Earth that are close to the sun, and giant cold worlds with deep atmospheres that lie far from the sun. The first probe to explore a giant planet was NASA's Pioneer 10. It flew past Jupiter, the largest planet of all, in 1973. Its twin probe, Pioneer 11, flew by Jupiter again the next year and then visited Saturn in 1979.

The planets all take different times to orbit the sun and, every few thousand years, they line up. The last time this happened was in the 1970s, and the U.S. decided use this opportunity to send new probes to explore some of them. Between them, the twin Voyager probes explored all four gas giants: Jupiter, Saturn, Uranus, and Neptune.

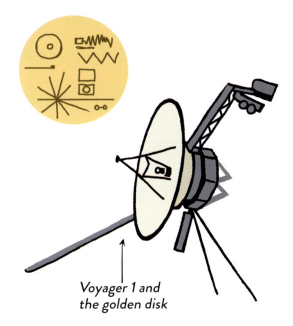

After their explorations of the solar system were complete, all these probes continued their journeys into interstellar space, and in many thousands of years they may pass close to other stars. In case they are encountered by any alien civilizations, the Pioneer probes have plaques on their sides, showing where they come from and what human beings look like. The Voyagers contain golden discs with sounds and images from Earth.

Voyager 1 and the golden disk

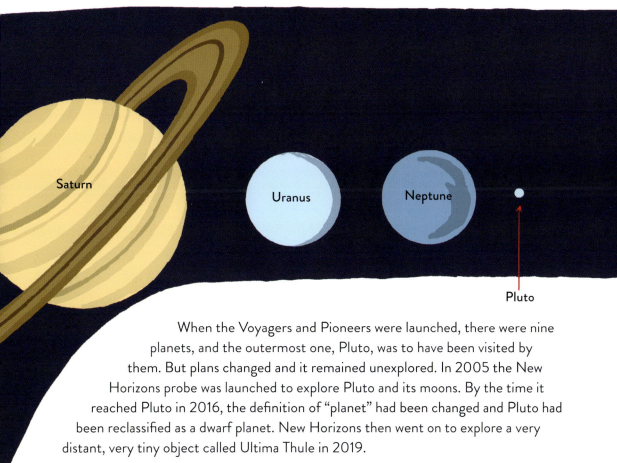

When the Voyagers and Pioneers were launched, there were nine planets, and the outermost one, Pluto, was to have been visited by them. But plans changed and it remained unexplored. In 2005 the New Horizons probe was launched to explore Pluto and its moons. By the time it reached Pluto in 2016, the definition of "planet" had been changed and Pluto had been reclassified as a dwarf planet. New Horizons then went on to explore a very distant, very tiny object called Ultima Thule in 2019.

New Eyes on the Universe

The light that we can see and the radio waves that cell phones use are two types of radiation. There are many more, including the X-rays that doctors use to peer inside us and the ultraviolet (UV) rays that cause sunburn. Together, all the different types of radiation make up the electromagnetic spectrum.

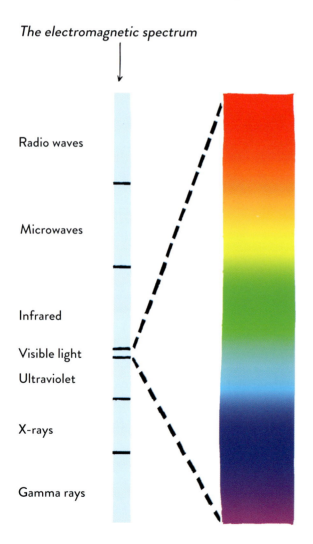

The electromagnetic spectrum

- Radio waves
- Microwaves
- Infrared
- Visible light
- Ultraviolet
- X-rays
- Gamma rays

Stars and other objects in space produce every kind of radiation, but most is blocked by Earth's atmosphere. So, to find out more about the universe, scientists in the late 20th century began to send telescopes above the atmosphere, on satellites.

The first successful space telescope was Uhuru, an X-ray telescope that discovered what was later proved to be a black hole. Many others followed, until every kind of radiation had at least one satellite to study it. As a result, our understanding of the universe increased greatly.

Even a telescope that uses ordinary light works better in space. There is no air to make the light from stars wobble, observations can be made at any time of day or night, and there are never clouds in the way. The most successful space telescope of this kind so far is the Hubble Space Telescope. Named after the astronomer Edwin Hubble (1889–1953), it was launched in 1990 and is still in use today. In December 2021, NASA launched the James Webb Space Telescope to study the universe.

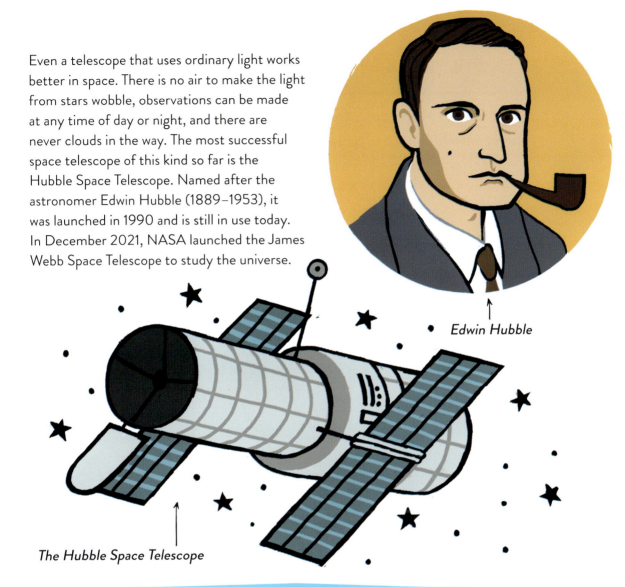

Edwin Hubble

The Hubble Space Telescope

Gravitational Waves

Meanwhile, on Earth, new kinds of telescope have been built; one type detects gravitational waves, which are produced by some of the most violent events in the universe, such as the crashing together of supermassive stars. Gravitational waves can tell us more about the beginning of the universe and about very distant events in space than any other kind of telescope, but these waves are very weak and have only been detected in the last few years.

A Home in Orbit

By the late 1960s, both the U.S. and the Soviet Union had put many satellites into orbit, and they both realized that the next step was to develop a satellite with people on board — a space station.

The first space station, the Soviet Salyut 1, was launched in 1971. Its three-man crew lived on board for 23 days, but the mission ended in disaster: oxygen escaped from the Soyuz 11 spacecraft that was taking the men back to Earth and tragically all of them died.

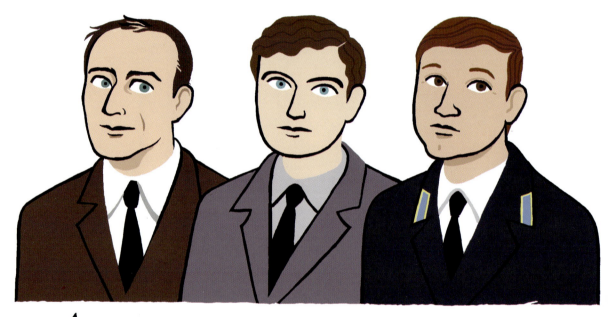

↑ *The crew of Soyuz 11, from left to right: Viktor Patsayev (1933–71), Vladislav Volkov (1935–71), and Georgy Dobrovolsky (1928–71)*

In 1973, the U.S. Skylab space station was launched; it was actually a converted section of a Saturn V rocket (see pages 18–19). It was occupied for 23 weeks, while the scientists on board studied the sun and the effects of orbital life on their own bodies. The astronauts returned safely, but Skylab crashed back to Earth in 1979; some parts fell onto the Australian Outback.

Weight Limit

There is a limit to the weight that a single rocket can launch, so large space stations must be assembled in orbit from sections sent up on separate flights. The first station of this kind was the Soviet Mir station; the first section was launched in 1986, the last in 1989. Mir was inhabited for 12 years.

In 1998, another new kind of station began to be built in orbit. The International Space Station (ISS) is a multinational project involving funds and technology from 16 countries. It has been growing larger ever since. It has been continuously in use since 2000, for scientific research and the study of new industrial techniques. It has even been used as a hotel for the first space tourists and it may one day become a launch platform for the first manned missions to Mars.

The ISS orbits Earth once every 90 (or so) minutes — which is around 16 times every 24 hours.

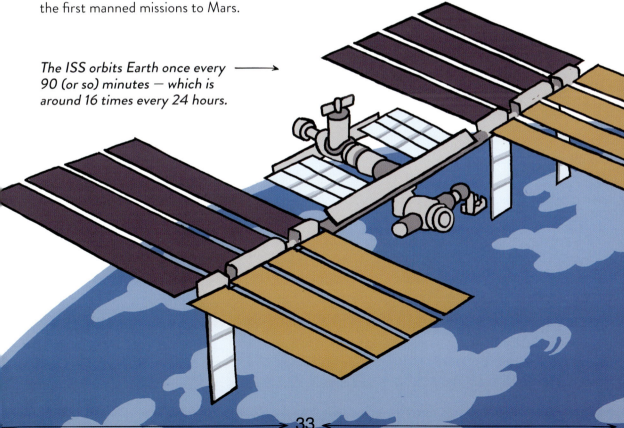

Space Shuttle

Until the 1980s, every spacecraft could be used only once, which made space travel extremely expensive. So, in 1981, a new kind of craft called a space shuttle was launched that could be reused many times. It took off using rockets but returned to Earth like a plane.

The part of the shuttle in which the crew traveled was called the orbiter. For launch, it was fitted with a large external tank and two smaller booster rockets. The orbiters had large cargo bays that could carry satellites, and some had robotic arms to lift these satellites out.

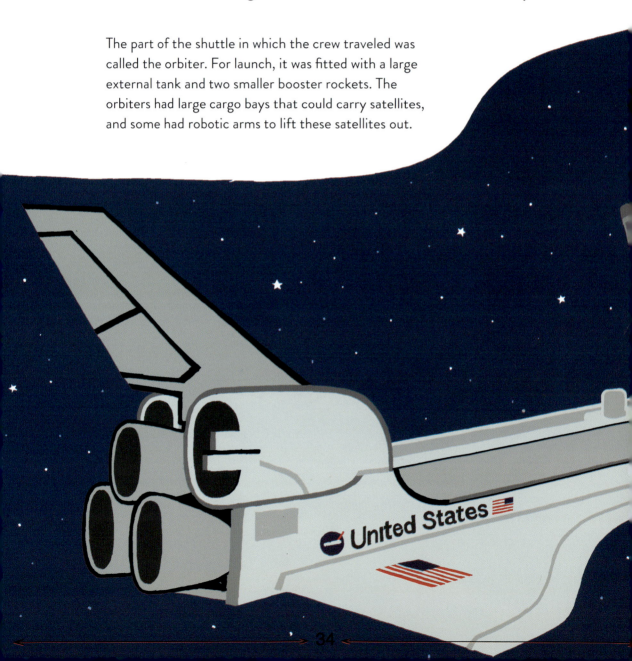

Five shuttles were used to carry satellites into orbit and to take parts, crews, and supplies to space stations (see pages 32–33). Another shuttle, called *Enterprise*, was built as a test vehicle and did not travel in space. Every shuttle could carry a crew of seven.

The most challenging shuttle mission was in 1993, when *Endeavour* repaired the faulty Hubble Space Telescope. Most missions were successful, but two ended tragically, killing their crews. In 1986, *Challenger* broke up soon after launch, and in 2003, one of *Columbia*'s wings was damaged during launch and caused the shuttle to disintegrate on re-entry. The final shuttle flight was made in 2011; it was the 135th mission.

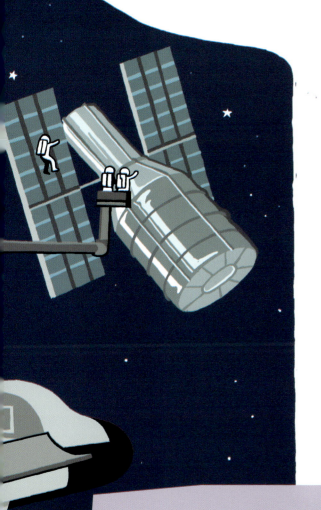

Space shuttle Endeavour's *robotic arm holds the Hubble Space Telescope as the crew repairs it.*

Soviet Shuttle

The Soviet Union had its own shuttle called Buran, which made a successful but unmanned orbital test flight in 1988. However, three years later the Soviet Union broke up into separate countries and Buran never made a crewed flight.

Journey to Jupiter

Jupiter is the largest planet in our solar system, and it has dozens of moons. Close-up views of the largest ones, as well as of Jupiter itself, were obtained by the Pioneer and Voyager missions in the 1970s. The moons were flown by again by the Ulysses sun probe in 1992, Cassini (on its way to Saturn — see pages 38–39) in 2000, and New Horizons on its way to Pluto in 2007 (see page 29).

Named after the first person to discover Jupiter's four largest moons, the first spacecraft to orbit Jupiter was Galileo, which arrived in 1995. Jupiter has a very deep and stormy atmosphere, which Galileo studied by launching a probe that fell slowly down through it. The probe sent signals back as it descended, reporting steadily increasing temperatures and pressures.

After nearly an hour, the probe reached a depth where the pressure was 23 times that on Earth and the temperature was 307°F (153°C). It stopped signaling at that point and must have melted soon afterward.

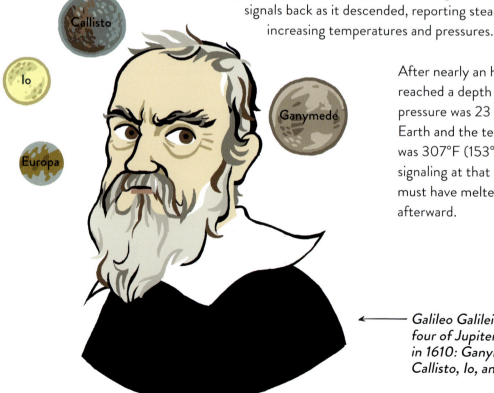

Galileo Galilei discovered four of Jupiter's moons in 1610: Ganymede, Callisto, Io, and Europa.

One of Jupiter's moons, Europa, has a liquid sea under its frozen surface, which may be home to living creatures. In case Galileo was carrying germs from Earth, NASA wanted to be quite sure the spacecraft did not, some time in the far future, crash onto Europa and spread its germs there. So, in 2003, Galileo was steered into Jupiter, where it was destroyed by the dense, hot, and stormy atmosphere.

The Galileo spacecraft makes its final descent into Jupiter's violent atmosphere.

Juno

Juno, the most recent visitor to Jupiter, went into orbit in 2016 and traveled over Jupiter's poles for the first time. It was the first spacecraft to observe Jupiter's south pole.

Saturn's Secrets

Many people think that Saturn, with its many moons and colorful rings, is the most beautiful planet of all. Its largest moon, Titan, is one of the most mysterious worlds in the solar system because its thick, cloudy atmosphere always hides its surface.

Like Jupiter, Saturn is a giant planet, with a thick atmosphere that is very cold on the outside, but very hot at lower levels. Saturn is the lightest planet for its size, light enough to float in water. It was flown past by Pioneer 11 and by both Voyager probes.

In 2004 a joint NASA/ESA mission arrived at Saturn to study both it and Titan. NASA's Cassini spacecraft went into orbit and began a detailed study of Saturn's many moons and complex ring system.

Saturn's rings are mainly made up of pieces of ice, with some dust and rock.

A few months later the ESA Huygens probe, which was ferried to Saturn by Cassini, was released to fall slowly through the atmosphere of Titan and land on its surface. It found a strange world of black lakes, yellowish clouds, and an atmosphere like that on Earth billions of years ago.

Titan

Rhea

Dione

Enceladus

Saturn has over 80 moons, more than any other planet in the solar system.

In 2017, Cassini completed its mission with a slow fall through Saturn's atmosphere. The harsh conditions destroyed it, but it continued to radio information back to Earth until its last moments, providing details about the strange chemicals it encountered.

New Ways to Space

In the 20th century, crewed spacecraft were built only by the governments of large countries. But in the 21st century, new inventions mean that private companies can afford to build spacecraft themselves. Meanwhile, many small countries have begun their own space programs.

The first crewed spacecraft that was not funded by a government was SpaceShipOne, which was launched on June 21, 2004. SpaceShipOne was a reusable craft and made two more short flights to the edge of space.

SpaceShipOne

Smartphones now contain such advanced technology, and are so tough, that they can be transformed into satellites. STRaND-1 (Surrey Training, Research and Nanosatellite Demonstrator 1) was the first such satellite, launched into orbit by an Indian rocket in 2013. As well as using the smartphone to carry out some of its tasks, the tiny (less than 11 pounds [5 kg]) satellite is trying out two new kinds of thrusters too. (Thrusters are the devices that change the direction of a spacecraft.)

Not all private spacecraft are small. A U.S. company called SpaceX has developed a rocket called Falcon Heavy, which is twice as powerful as the space shuttle's launch system was. In February 2018, Falcon Heavy was used to launch a Tesla Roadster (an electric car) into orbit around the sun.

Falcon Heavy blasts off

Space Dragons

In 2019 Crew Dragon, another SpaceX spacecraft, docked with the International Space Station. This was a test mission, as Crew Dragon had no one on board and was controlled from Earth. But future flights will ferry astronauts to and from the ISS.

The Future in Space

In the next ten years, we can expect to see more men and women landing on the moon, while robot spacecraft explore the asteroid belt, which is an area of space between Mars and Jupiter that contains many tiny worlds.

A NASA probe called OSIRIS-Rex arrived at an asteroid called Bennu, and in 2023 it brought a sample back to Earth. Soon after, other asteroids might be sampled by a probe called Prospector 1. If it finds precious minerals, larger spacecraft may be sent to mine these asteroids or even tow them back to Earth.

Many countries have wanted to send people to Mars, but the enormous distance involved (more than 140 times the distance to the moon) makes this a very challenging project. The first crewed missions will probably take astronauts into Martian orbit, as this is simpler and safer than landing them on Mars. Meanwhile, robots may be sent to Mars to prepare a landing site and base for later missions.

A spacecraft towing an asteroid

More advanced telescopes will be launched into space over the next few decades. The James Webb Space Telescope (JWST) was launched in December 2021. It has an enormous mirror measuring 21 feet (6.5 m) across to detect infrared radiation from distant stars and planets.

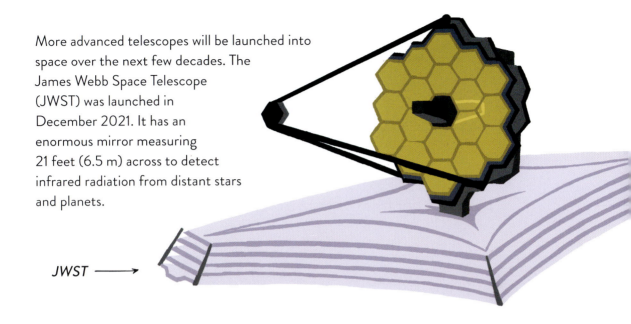

JWST ⟶

James E. Webb

James E. Webb (1906–92) ran the NASA space agency from 1961 to 1968. He was appointed by President John F. Kennedy (see page 16) and was a key figure in the Apollo Space Program (see pages 20–21).

James E. ⟶
Webb

In about 2034 a trio of satellites will be launched to study black holes. These are the dead remains of huge stars, with gravity so strong that not even light can escape from them and any passing spacecraft would be pulled down and destroyed. The satellites work by detecting radiation called gravitational waves.

Starships

To reach a star, a spacecraft needs no more fuel than to reach any other planet of our solar system; once it is well away from the gravitational pull of the sun, it will continue on until it is either destroyed or reaches a new world. But no space probe has yet visited a star, simply because stars are so far away. The nearest star (other than the sun) is a million times farther from us than Venus, the nearest planet.

Star Encounters

The Pioneer, Voyager, and New Horizons probes are all speeding toward distant stars. The fastest is Voyager 1, which is traveling at 10.5 miles (17 km) per second. But it will not encounter a star for many thousands of years.

To reach a star in a short time requires very high speeds. The simplest way to achieve them is to build a very lightweight space probe. It might be possible to build one weighing less than an ounce, containing a tiny camera and transmitter.

Rather than carrying fuel with it, this kind of probe would be pushed through space by the light from powerful lasers based on Earth. It is thought that a probe like this might be launched around 2035 and reach the nearest star about 50 years later.

← An artist's impression of a laser-powered space probe

Getting people to the planets of other stars will be much harder. One possible way is by using nuclear fusion (the same process that keeps the sun shining), but even then, the journeys would take decades. It might be that the crews could spend most of that time in specially designed pods in a state of hibernation, like bears or tortoises.

↑
An artist's impression of a hibernation pod

The possibilities of space exploration are endless. Many of the inventions we take for granted today were unimaginable a century ago, and many scientists used to believe that human space travel was impossible. Perhaps we will learn completely new ways of traveling though space, or perhaps we will meet travelers from other worlds and explore the universe with them. One day, you may become a space traveler yourself.

Glossary

asteroid A tiny, rocky world. Most are found in an area called the asteroid belt, between Mars and Jupiter. They are probably leftovers of the material from which the planets formed.

astronaut (also cosmonaut) A space traveler.

atmosphere The layer of gases that surrounds a planet or star. Beyond the atmosphere, space begins. Small worlds, such as asteroids and most moons, don't have atmospheres.

crater A bowl-shaped feature found on the surface of a rocky planet or moon. Some are dead volcanoes, and others are caused by the impact of space rocks, such as asteroids.

gravity The force that pulls you to Earth and keeps Earth and the other planets in orbit around the sun.

gunpowder A mixture of chemicals that is used to make explosives, such as fireworks.

hibernation When an animal sleeps very deeply for weeks or even months.

infrared Invisible radiation given off by stars and other hot objects.

laser Short for Light Amplification by Stimulated Emission of Radiation, this light travels in straight lines and makes a very narrow and very bright beam of light.

lunar To do with the moon.

moon A world that orbits a planet.

nuclear fusion The process that happens deep inside the sun to produce sunlight. It can also be used to make powerful bombs.

orbit The path of one object around another in space, such as a planet traveling around a star.

planet A large world that orbits a star.

probe (short for space probe) A spacecraft with no crew that is sent to explore other worlds and send information back to Earth.

radiation (short for electromagnetic radiation) Energy that is sent out by all hot objects and many other things too. Light, infrared, ultraviolet, and radio waves are all types of radiation.

radio waves Radiation that we can use to communicate via cell phones, satellites, and other devices. Radio waves are produced naturally by many objects in space.

satellite A spacecraft with no crew that orbits Earth or another world; moons are natural satellites.

solar To do with the sun.

solar system The sun together with all the planets, moons, asteroids, comets, and other objects that orbit it.

stage (of a rocket) A part of a rocket that contains fuel tanks and that can be discarded when the fuel is used up.

ultraviolet Invisible radiation given off by hot objects that can tan and burn the skin.

Further Information

Books

A Guide to Space
by Kevin Pettman (Wayland, 2020)

Cats React to Outer Space Facts
by Izzi Howell (Wayland, 2020)

Go Quiz Yourself!: Space
by Izzi Howell (Wayland, 2020)

Infomojis: Space
by Jon Richards and Ed Simkins
(Wayland, 2019)

Out of This World Space Tech
by Clive Gifford (Cavendish Square, 2024)

Space Explorers
by Libby Jackson and Léonard Dupond
(Wren & Rook, 2020)

Note to parents and teachers: Every effort has been made by the Publishers to ensure that the websites in this book are of the highest educational value, and that they contain no inappropriate or offensive material. However, because of the nature of the Internet, it is impossible to guarantee that the contents of these sites will not be altered. We strongly advise that Internet access is supervised by a responsible adult.

Websites

www.esa.int
The kids section of the European Space Agency website is packed with fun facts and activities.

www.markthompsonastronomy.com
Mark is an astronomer, television presenter, and author on all things space-related. His website is packed with practical tips on astronomy and lots of facts about the solar system.

www.nasa.gov
Browse the NASA website to read about the amazing history of space exploration and to see incredible photographs of planets, rockets, and deep space. You can also find out when the ISS is passing over your town or city to try to spot it in the night sky, and you can watch live launches and landings of astronauts to and from the ISS.

www.worldspaceweek.org
Visit this site to see when World Space Week will take place each year and to find out about any local events taking place that you can join in with.

Places to visit

National Air and Space Museum
Washington, D.C.
https://airandspace.si.edu

Kennedy Space Center
Merritt Island, FL
https://kennedyspacecenter.com

Cosmosphere Space Museum
Hutchinson, KS
https://cosmo.org

Intrepid Sea, Air, and Space Museum
New York, NY
https://intrepidmuseum.org

Space Center Houston
Houston, TX
https://spacecenter.org

San Diego Air and Space Museum
San Diego, CA
https://sandiegoairandspace.org

INDEX

Apollo Space Program 20, 21, 43
asteroid belt 42
astronauts 12, 13, 14, 17, 19, 21, 32, 41, 42
    Aldrin, Buzz 21
    Armstrong, Neil 21
    Collins, Michael 21
    Dobrovolsky, Georgy 32
    Gagarin, Yuri 12, 13
    Glenn, John 13
    Leonov, Alexei 13
    Patsayev, Viktor 32
    Shepard, Alan 13
    Tereshkova, Valentina 12, 13
    Volkov, Vladislav 32
    White, Ed 13
atmospheres 8, 9, 14, 18, 27, 28, 30, 36, 37, 38, 39

black holes 30, 43

China 5
Cold War 10, 16
cosmic rays 9
cosmonauts (*see astronauts*)
craters 24, 25, 27

electromagnetic spectrum 30
England 7, 8
European Space Agency (ESA) 25, 27, 38, 39

Galilei, Galileo 6, 7, 36
Gemini program 17
Germany 8
Global Positioning System 15
Goddard, Robert 5
gravity 24, 43

Hubble, Edwin 31

infrared rays 7, 30

Japanese Aerospace Exploration Agency 25
Jupiter 6, 7, 28, 36–37, 38, 42

Kazakhstan 12
Kennedy, President John F. 16, 43

Laika (dog) 11

Magellan, Ferdinand 27
Mars 7, 22–23, 33, 28, 42
Mercury (planet) 7, 24–25
Mercury, Project 13
moon, the 4, 6, 16, 17, 18, 20–21, 42
moons 6, 29, 36, 37, 38, 39

NASA 13, 14, 16, 17, 18, 19, 24, 26, 28, 37, 38, 42, 43
Neptune 7, 28, 29
Newton, Isaac 6

planets 4, 7, 14, 22, 24, 26, 27, 28, 29, 36, 38, 39, 43, 44, 45
Pluto 29, 36
probes 16, 17, 22, 23, 24, 25, 26, 27, 28, 29, 36, 38, 39, 42, 44

radiation 7, 11, 14, 30, 43
radio waves 30
robot rovers 23
robots 42
rockets 5, 8–9, 11, 12, 18–19, 21, 32, 33, 34, 41
    Aerobees 9
    Falcon Heavy 41
    Saturn Vs 18–19, 21, 32
    V-2s 8, 9

satellites 10, 11, 12, 14–15, 30, 32, 34, 35, 41, 43
    Sputnik (1&2) 10, 11, 12

Saturn 7, 28, 38–39
smartphones 41
solar system 7, 22, 26, 28, 29, 36, 38, 39, 44
Soviet Union 10, 12, 16, 35
space shuttle 35–36, 41
space stations 32, 33, 35, 41
    ISS 33, 41
    Mir 33
    Salyut 1 32
    Skylab 32
spacecraft 4, 8, 10, 12, 13, 16, 17, 18, 21, 22, 24, 32, 34, 36, 37, 38, 40, 41, 42, 43, 44
SpaceShipOne 40
spacesuits 19
spacewalks 13, 17
SpaceX 41
stars 4, 6, 7, 14, 29, 30, 31, 43, 44
sun 4, 14, 24, 25, 28, 32, 41, 44, 45

telescopes 6, 7, 14, 30, 31, 35, 43
    Hubble Space Telescope 31, 35
    James Webb Space Telescope 43
    Lovell Telescope, Jodrell Bank 7
    Uhuru telescope 30
Tsiolkovsky, Konstantin 5

Ultima Thule 29
ultraviolet (UV) rays 7, 14, 30
United States 8, 9, 10, 16, 21
universe 6, 7, 30–31, 45
Uranus 7, 26, 28

Van Allen belts 11
Van Allen, James 11
Venera 13 lander 26
Venus 7, 24, 25, 26–27, 44
Venus Express orbiter 27

World War II 8

48